For my two favorite explorers,
Andy and Allie

ISBN: 1-56476-571-7
1 2 3 4 5 6 7 8 9 10
Printing/Year 00 99 98 97 96
© 1996 by Michael Carroll. All rights reserved.
Printed in Mexico.
For more information write Victor Books,
1825 College Avenue, Wheaton, Illinois 60187.

Editor: Liz Duckworth
Designer: Scott Rattray
Production: Myrna Hasse

Paintings by Michael Carroll
Photo Credits:
Page 9, Solar flare (Skylab photo courtesy NASA); The Sun (NASA)
Page 11, Mercury (NASA/JPL)
Page 12, Venus (C.L. Esposito and NASA)
Page 12, Venus, surface (The Russian Space Agency [RKA] and NASA/JPL)
Page 13, Venus, mountain (NASA/JPL)
Page 14, Earth view (NASA)
Page 17, Mars (c. Philip James, Steven Lee, and NASA)
Page 19, Jupiter (Voyager 1, NASA/JPL)
Page 25, Uranus (Voyager 2, NASA/JPL)
Page 26, Neptune (Voyager 2, NASA/JPL)
Page 29, Pluto and Charon (c. Dr. R. Albrecht, ESA/ESO Space
          Telescope European Coordination Facility/NASA)

SPINNING
WORLDS

Michael Carroll

VICTOR BOOKS

A DIVISION OF SCRIPTURE PRESS PUBLICATIONS INC.
USA CANADA ENGLAND

CREATION

In the beginning, God created the heavens and the earth . . . And God said, "Let there be light," and there was light . . . and God saw that is was good. Genesis 1:1, 3, 10

A very long time ago, there was nothing. Then, God decided to make something out of nothing, and so He did! In the darkness, there was suddenly a great light, and everything that we know came into being.

God has created many amazing things and put them in a wonderfully big place, which we call the universe. The universe is filled with spinning planets, twirling galaxies, glowing stars, and . . . you! You are very important to God, so important that He made things around you to show you and everyone else just how great He is.

God has put people on the Earth to enjoy Him, and to enjoy His creation. All around the Earth, God has put other worlds. On these planets are the highest mountains, the deepest canyons, and the fiercest storms, all revealing the power of their Creator.

THE SUN

The sun has one kind of splendor, the moon another and the stars another; and star differs from star in splendor. 1 Corinthians 15:41

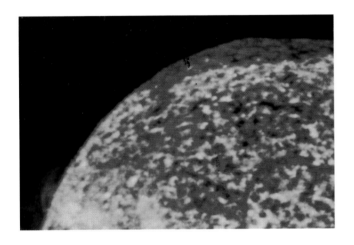

Our Sun is a gigantic burning ball of *hydrogen gas*—so big that over one million Earths could fit inside. The Sun is a star, like those God has sprinkled across the night sky. But our Sun is very close to Earth. God placed the Sun perfectly to heat and light our world.

The sun has great storms on it called *sunspots*. These storms throw hot material far into space in fiery tongues called *flares*. A stream of hot gas pours from the Sun.

Many worlds, comets, and asteroids circle around the Sun. They form a family—the *solar system*. Its nine worlds are called *planets*. Some of the bigger planets have moons, and some of these moons are actually larger than the smallest planets!

Top **The Sun seen through computer eyes. This picture was taken by the Skylab space station.**

Bottom **A giant solar flare explodes from the side of the Sun. Compare its size to the tiny dot, which is the size of our Earth.**

Opposite page **When the Moon comes between the Earth and Sun (called an *eclipse*), we can see the Sun's beautiful corona of light, and its pink solar flares.**

MERCURY

Now no one can look at the sun, bright as it is in the skies . . . Job 37:21

Above **Mercury is a battered, hot world. It is covered with craters. This view was snapped by the camera aboard the spacecraft Mariner 10.**

Opposite page **From Mercury, the Sun would look three times as big as it does in our sky. Some deep valleys may have ice.**

The closest planet to our sun is called Mercury. Mercury turns very slowly, so it has a long day. On the Earth, a day lasts 24 hours. On Mercury, it takes about 58 Earth days to turn around one time.

Mercury is so close to the Sun, it doesn't have as far to go around. So a year lasts only 88 days—much shorter than Earth's 365-day year!

Mercury has no air around it. Air acts like a blanket for a planet, keeping it warm at night, and cool during the day. Since Mercury has no blanket of air, it is extremely hot during the day. But at night it gets cold, even though it is right next to the Sun. Imagine—this is one world that is both too hot and too cold for people to live there!

Like the Moon in our sky, Mercury is covered with *craters,* or bowl-shaped pits. Craters are caused by *meteors* and *asteroids*—rocks which fly through space—which have hit the ground on Mercury. Mercury's mountains and long cliffs add beauty to this pitted planet.

Most of Venus is covered with deserts of sand and rock.

Inset to left This photo of Venus was taken by the Hubble Space Telescope. It shows the acid clouds covering the planet.

Inset to left Russian Venera lander photo of the surface of Venus

VENUS

. . .touch the mountains, so that they smoke. Send forth lightning . . . Psalm 144:5-6

The next planet out from the Sun is Venus. Venus is a twin of Earth in size, but it is a very different place. This is partly because of the air around it. Mercury does not have any blanket of air, but Venus has too much of one! Venus is covered with dense clouds. Because of its thick *atmosphere,* the ground on Venus is much hotter than

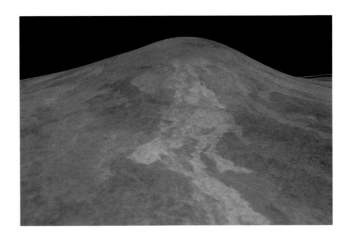

Magellan radar image of a mountain on Venus.

any kitchen oven. In fact, if you go on a picnic there, don't bring any silverware—it will melt!

We cannot see through the clouds of Venus, but we can map its surface using *radar beams.* We have also sent space probes through the clouds to see what it is like below. Under the clouds is a world where every day brings a dark yellow sky. Lightning crashes through the clouds, and slow winds brush across the sand and rock. There is rain on Venus, but it is not made of water. It is acid!

God covered the surface of this planet with deserts, mountains, and erupting volcanoes—but there is no life on Earth's stormy neighbor.

EARTH AND THE MOON

Who is this that appears like the dawn, fair as the moon, bright as the sun, majestic as the stars in procession?

Song of Songs 6:10

This beautiful photo was taken by the Apollo 8 astronauts while over the Moon. The Earth is rich and blue compared to the dead Moon. White clouds drift across the blue oceans and red land of Africa along the bottom edge.

The third planet from the Sun is our home. It is perfect for us. God covered Earth with something you will not find anywhere else in the entire solar system: liquid water! The Earth's atmosphere protects us from meteors and asteroids and gives us air to breathe. The air keeps us warm at night and cool during the day. God has made Earth just right to support the creatures He loves.

The Moon is the closest world to Earth, though it is much smaller. When it lights our nights, its light comes from the Sun shining off it. The moon circles the Earth once each month; you can see its shape change as it moves around our planet.

The Moon is a dead place with no atmosphere. It has high, smooth moutains, dusty plains, and many craters. Some craters are hundreds of miles across!

Besides the Earth, the Moon is the only other place people have visited. Twelve astronauts have explored the moon, taking pictures and bringing back rocks and dirt for scientists to study. The Moon, our closest space neighbor, is 240,000 miles (384,000 kilometers) away. God gave us this far-away light which often brightens dark nights.

An asteroid slams into Mars. Steam and dust float into the peach-colored sky. Sometimes asteroids have melted ice in the Martian ground, causing floods like we see in this painting.

MARS

Who cuts a channel for the torrents of rain, and a path for the thunderstorm, to water a land where no man lives, a desert with no one in it . . . Job 38:25-26

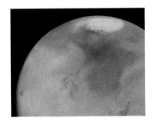

Mars is called the red planet, because of its brownish-red soil. In a telescope, you can see dark markings on Mars. When scientists sent robot spaceships to look at the red planet up close, we found out that these dark lines on Mars are volcanic dust. We have not found any life on this desert world.

What we have found is a cold place with thin, poisonous air. Mars has beautiful mountains, craters, and deep valleys carved by floods of water. There are smooth areas which look to some people like places where oceans used to be. But if Mars ever did have oceans, it became very cold and dry later. Today, most of its water is frozen at its north and south poles.

Things do not weigh as much on Mars as they do on the Earth. The smaller a planet is, the less *gravity* it has. Gravity is what holds us down. On Mars, you could jump three times as far as you can on Earth!

Mars has a giant volcano nearly three times as high as Earth's highest mountain. It has a huge canyon—far bigger than the Grand Canyon in the United States and five times as deep. God has made Mars as full of surprises as our own world is.

Top left **A long time ago, scientists thought there were creatures living on Mars. Some people thought the dark lines on Mars were canals built by "Martians."**

Top right **This photograph of Mars was taken by the Hubble Space Telescope. You can see the bright ice on the north pole, and the dark markings across its red deserts.**

JUPITER

He loads the clouds with moisture; he scatters his lightning through them. At his direction they swirl around . . . Job 37:11-12

Jupiter seen from Amalthea Jupiter's tiny moon Amalthea is only as far across as a city. From Amalthea, Jupiter's beautiful clouds would fill half of the sky.

All of the planets we have seen so far have had rocky ground. Mercury, Venus, Earth and Mars are called the *inner planets.* But beyond them are what we call the *outer planets.* They are very different.

Jupiter is the biggest planet in our solar system. If you took all the other planets and their moons and put them together, they would not weigh as much as Jupiter does. Jupiter could hold 1,300 Earths. Since Jupiter is so big, do you think you could jump very high there?

Above Two moons can be seen floating in front of Jupiter's colorful cloud bands. The orange moon on the left is Io, and the white moon is Europa. Jupiter's great red spot is behind them.

Jupiter is a big ball of gas. It has no solid ground to stand on. The clouds of Jupiter wrap around the planet in beautiful bands of yellow, brown, and white stripes. Within these bands are great storms, much like hurricanes on Earth. One of these storms, the Great Red Spot, is big enough to swallow two and a half Earths!

Powerful lightning bolts streak through the skies of Jupiter. The clouds are made of *ammonia* and water, and there is probably rain and hail beneath these clouds. Strong winds rip through the bands of this strange weather-world that God has wonderfully created.

JUPITER'S BIG MOONS

The mountains melt beneath him and the valleys split apart, like wax before the fire . . .

Micah 1:4

Icy Corridors of Europa Dark lines and icy ridges wander across Europa. Up in the sky we see giant Jupiter and orange Io.

Above **Jupiter and four of its seventeen moons.**

Center, Io Caldera **Io has many volcanic craters. From Io, Jupiter would be as far across as 39 full moons in Earth's sky!**

Bottom, Ganymede **Strange valleys cut across the frozen ground of *Ganymede*. Here, we see a crater which has been split in half by the movement of the ground.**

Seventeen moons orbit Jupiter. Most are small, but four are very big as moons go. The strange beauty of Io, Europa, Ganymede, and Callisto points to the amazing and creative God who shaped our universe.

Jupiter is so far from the Sun that astronomers expected its moons to be icy. They were right about Europa, Ganymede, and Callisto. These three moons are balls of ice frozen as hard as rock.

Europa looks like a giant cracked egg. Some people think there may be an ocean of water beneath Europa's frozen surface.

Ganymede is Jupiter's biggest moon. It is covered with craters which have melted away on its soft ice surface. Big canyons wind across the face of this blue and tan moon. These canyons slice through mountains and craters as if a giant took a fork and scraped the surface.

Callisto is frozen harder than Europa or Ganymede. Its brown face is completely covered with old craters.

God had a surprise for scientists when they saw Io. Instead of being frozen, Io is covered with volcanoes. Io is pushed and pulled by Jupiter and the other three large moons, so its insides heat up. The heat comes out as volcanic eruptions, sailing high into Io's airless sky.

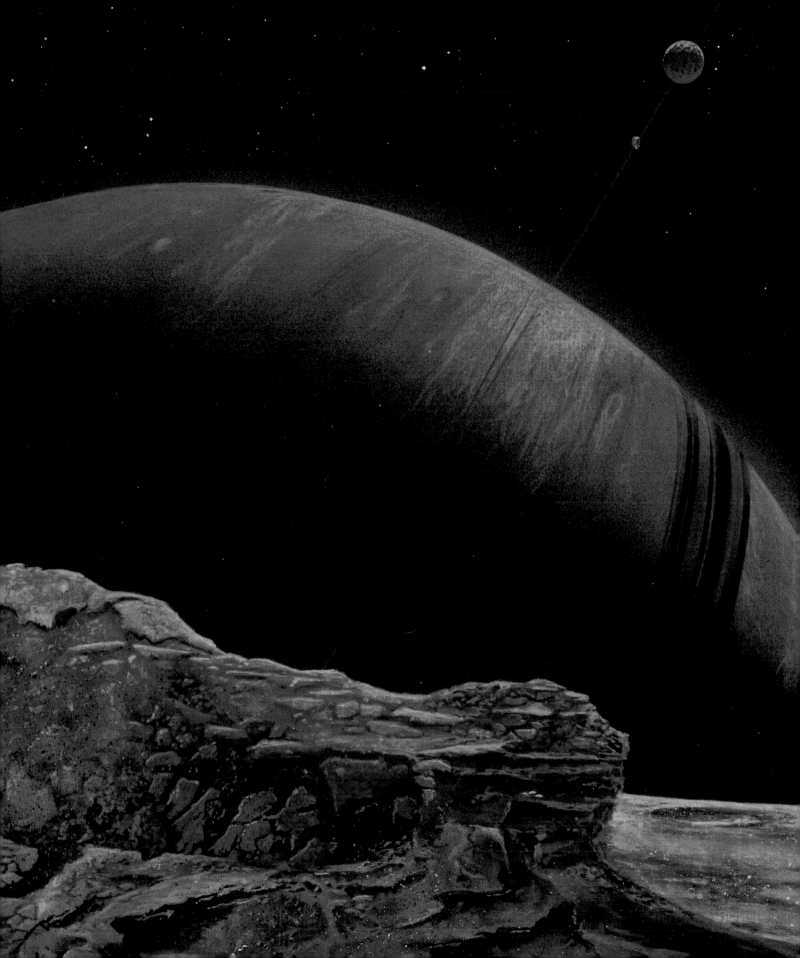

SATURN

He overlaid it with pure gold. . . He cast four gold rings for it . . . Exodus 37:2-3

Spinning through space like a golden top is Saturn, the ringed giant. Saturn's tan and yellow clouds stretch around it much like the bands of Jupiter do, but Saturn's clouds are not as colorful. Saturn has great storms and a deep atmosphere much like that of Jupiter.

The most amazing thing about Saturn is its rings. Saturn has thousands of rings, too many to count. The rings are not solid. They are made of dust, ice, and boulders that float around the planet in a big, flat disk. Some of the rings are as thin as smoke, while others have boulders the size of compact cars. God has given Saturn the biggest rings of any planet in our solar system.

Saturn is nearly as big as Jupiter, but it is much lighter. In fact, if you could fill a big enough bathtub with water, and you put Saturn in it, the planet would float!

Saturn has the most moons of any planet. There are at least 23. Some are potato-shaped and small, while others are round balls of ice. None of the moons are as big as Jupiter's four large moons, except for Titan.

Above Saturn's strange black and white moon, Iapetus, has a wonderful view of Saturn in its sky.

Left page Many of Saturn's moons are balls of ice. Enceladus is one of these. From Enceladus Saturn's rings look like a thin line in the sky because they are even with Enceladus' orbit around Saturn. Another moon, Mimas, is in the sky.

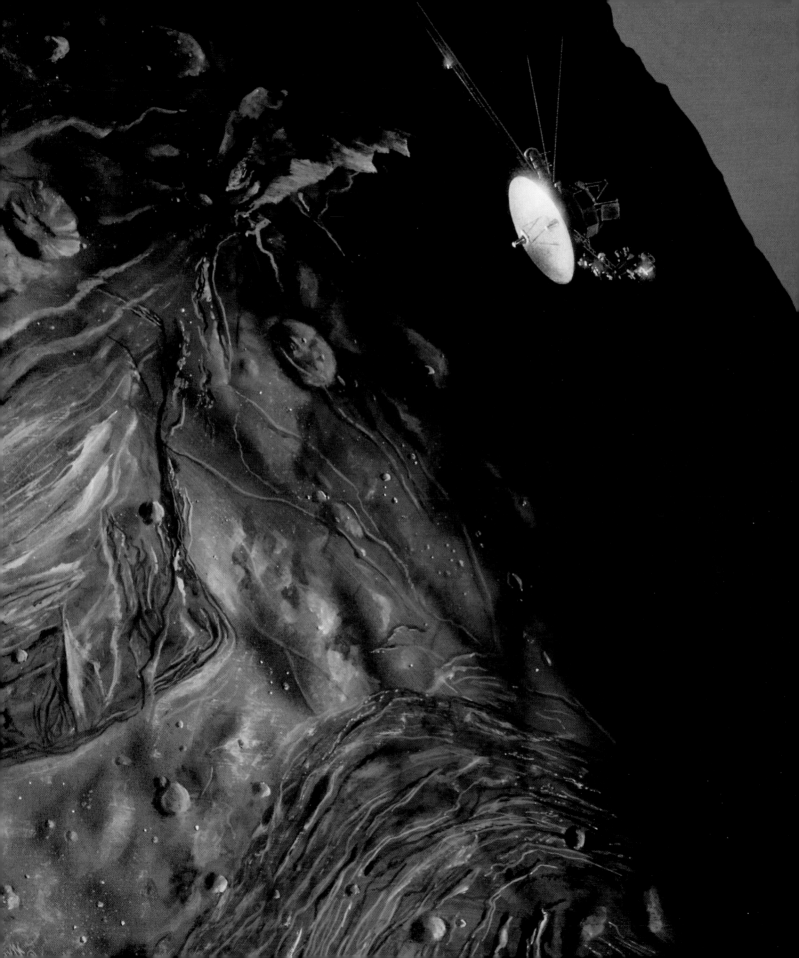

URANUS

It is close at hand—a day of darkness and gloom, a day of clouds and blackness. Joel 2:1-2

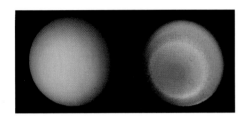

Easter egg or planet? The picture on the left shows what Uranus really looks like. The one on the right was done by a computer to show us the cloud bands under Uranus' green fog. Uranus has cloud bands just like Jupiter and Saturn, but they are hard to see without a computer.

Beyond Saturn, the Sun begins to look less like a yellow ball and more like a bright star. Out here in the gloom lies the seventh planet, Uranus.

Uranus is a gas giant—the same kind of planet as Jupiter, Saturn, and Neptune. All four have cloudy bands and rings, though some rings are hard to see. Uranus' rings are made of black rock, sand, and ice, so they are almost invisible.

Unlike any other planet in our Sun's family, Uranus spins around on its side. This planet has been called the Jolly Green Giant. It is big enough to swallow 15 Earths, and its green fog comes from a gas called *methene.*

Uranus has 15 moons that we know of. Most are small, rocky bodies, but the five biggest have icy surfaces. They are called Miranda, Ariel, Umbriel, Titania, and Oberon. The strangest of these is Miranda. Miranda is small, and its surface seems to be all mixed up. It has mountains and craters, but it also has round plains that look like racetracks. Scientists think Miranda was hit by a huge cosmic rock and mixed up before it froze into the moon we see today—another of God's surprises!

Painting, left **In 1986 Voyager 2 flew very close to Uranus and its strange little moon, Miranda.**

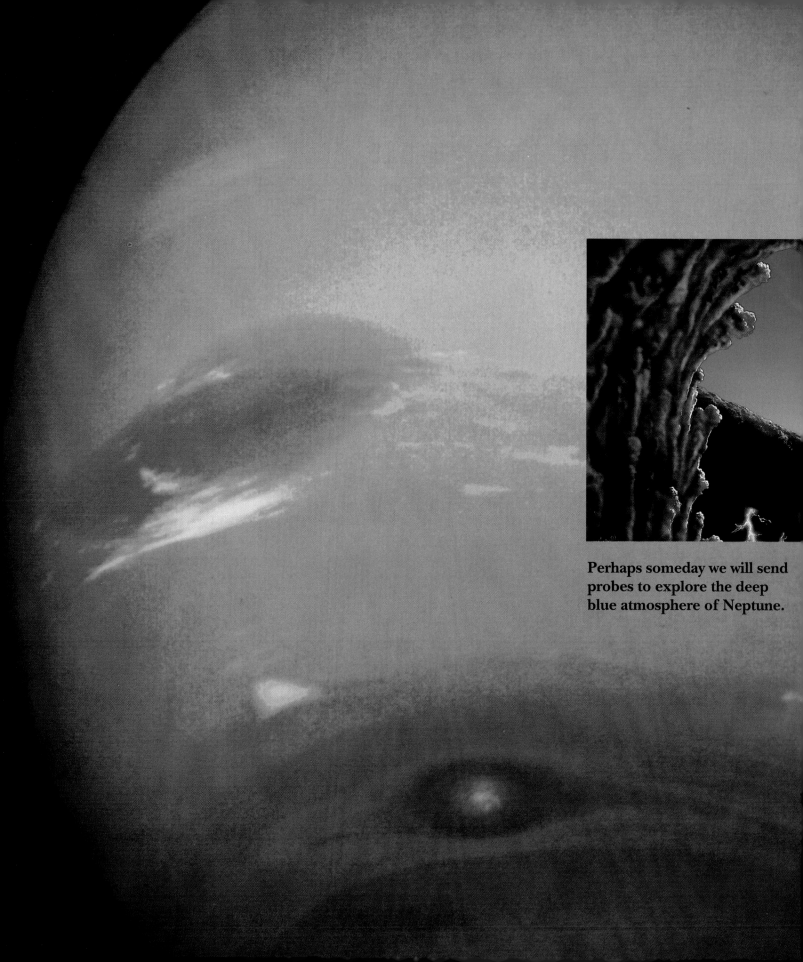

Perhaps someday we will send probes to explore the deep blue atmosphere of Neptune.

NEPTUNE

Lightning and hail, snow and clouds, stormy winds that do his bidding . . . Psalm 148:8

Before scientists got their first close look at Neptune, they thought it would be a boring place. They knew Neptune is so far from the Sun that it is very cold, so they supposed Neptune's clouds would be very quiet. But as often happens, God's creation is more wonderful than our minds can imagine!

Neptune turned out to be a very exciting place with storms the size of the Earth and cold winds that are stronger than on any other planet. Neptune is a beautiful sky-blue color with dark blue storms and white clouds. It has its own heat inside, though where this heat comes from is still a mystery.

When the Voyager 2 spacecraft sent us the first close-up pictures of Neptune, a great storm spread across the blue clouds. They called it the Great Blue Spot, because it reminded them of Jupiter's Great Red Spot. But Neptune's blue storm disappeared in a year. The Hubble Space Telescope shows us that new storms are forming there even now.

Neptune is so far from the Sun that it takes 165 years to go once around! Its day lasts about 16 hours, and it is the same size as Uranus.

Like the other gas giants, Neptune has many moons. There are at least eight, and one of them is a strange world indeed. It is called Triton.

Two blue storms can be seen in this photo of Neptune. The biggest one is the size of the Earth.

Pluto and Charon

Hubble Space Telescope
Faint Object Camera

This photo is the best picture ever taken of Pluto. The smaller dot is Pluto's moon, Charon. Pluto is so small and far away that taking this picture was like taking picture of a baseball 40 miles (64 km) away!

TRITON AND PLUTO: COSMIC TWINS?

*He who turns dawn to darkness, and treads the high places . . .
the Lord God Almighty is his name.* Amos 4:13

Neptune's moon *Triton* is a frozen little world. Most of the air you are breathing right now is *nitrogen,* but Triton is so cold that nitrogen freezes and falls to the ground as pink ice! The air on Triton is very thin.

Triton has volcanoes made of ice. Instead of lava, these mountains erupt frozen water. Black geysers of nitrogen fog shoot from the ground and drift in the thin winds. Strange waves of ice water have flooded the moon's landscape, wiping out any craters that might have been there.

Neptune's moon Triton is about the same size as the farthest planet out from the Sun, *Pluto.* Many scientists believe that Pluto and Triton look a lot alike. We have not seen Pluto up close, but we know it has a thin atmosphere and that it is about as big and cold as Triton. Pluto has a moon called *Charon.* The Hubble Space Telescope has taken the best photos of Pluto and its moon, but even these show only fuzzy dots.

Someday, scientists hope to send a spacecraft to Pluto so we can see what this distant world looks like up close.

Ice volcanoes on Triton send smoke into the thin air. Neptune is seen in the sky.

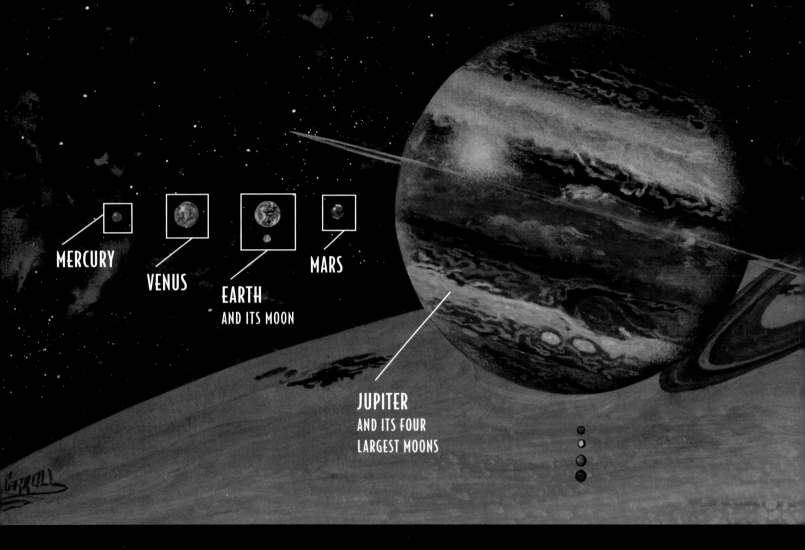

MERCURY

VENUS

EARTH
AND ITS MOON

MARS

JUPITER
AND ITS FOUR
LARGEST MOONS

Glossary

Asteroid: a chunk of rock and metal.

Astronomer: a person who studies outer space.

Atmosphere: the air around a planet or moon.

Comet: a ball of rock and ice which orbits around the Sun. As a comet warms up, it melts, developing a beautiful tail stretching far out into space.

Corona: the Sun's atmosphere, a stream of hot gas which forms a glowing crown around the Sun.

Crater: a bowl-shaped pit in a planet or moon caused by the crash of an asteroid, meteoroid or comet. Some craters are also made by volcanoes.

Day: the time it takes for a planet or moon to spin around once (or, the time between one sunrise and another).

Flare: a fiery explosion thrown out from the Sun.